CW00346905

CHRIS HANNAN

Chris Hannan's previous work has been produced by the Royal Shakespeare Company and by Sir Peter Hall at the Old Vic. *The Evil Doers* won a Time Out Award and the Charrington London Fringe Best Play Award when first seen at the Bush Theatre, and he was nominated Lloyds Bank Playwright of the Year for *Shining Souls* in 1996. Five of his plays have premiered at the Traverse Theatre, Edinburgh, including the contemporary classic *Elizabeth Gordon Quinn,* which was revived by the National Theatre of Scotland in its inaugural 2006 season. His 2010 play for children and families *The Three Musketeers and the Princess of Spain* won five star reviews in England and a Scottish Critics' CATS Award for Best New Play.

His debut novel *Missy* was awarded the 2009 McKitterick Prize by the Society of Authors.

Other Titles in this Series

Howard Brenton
ANNE BOLEYN
BERLIN BERTIE
FAUST – PARTS ONE & TWO
    after Goethe
IN EXTREMIS
NEVER SO GOOD
PAUL
THE RAGGED TROUSERED
    PHILANTHROPISTS *after* Tressell

Caryl Churchill
BLUE HEART
CHURCHILL PLAYS: THREE
CHURCHILL PLAYS: FOUR
CHURCHILL: SHORTS
CLOUD NINE
A DREAM PLAY
    after Strindberg
DRUNK ENOUGH TO SAY
    I LOVE YOU?
FAR AWAY
HOTEL
ICECREAM
LIGHT SHINING IN
    BUCKINGHAMSHIRE
MAD FOREST
A NUMBER
SEVEN JEWISH CHILDREN
THE SKRIKER
THIS IS A CHAIR
THYESTES *after* Seneca
TRAPS

Ariel Dorfman
DEATH AND THE MAIDEN
PURGATORIO
READER
THE RESISTANCE TRILOGY
WIDOWS

Helen Edmundson
ANNA KARENINA *after* Tolstoy
THE CLEARING
CORAM BOY *after* Gavin
GONE TO EARTH *after* Webb
LIFE IS A DREAM *after* Calderón
THE MILL ON THE FLOSS
    after Eliot
MOTHER TERESA IS DEAD
ORESTES *after* Euripides
WAR AND PEACE *after* Tolstoy

Debbie Tucker Green
BORN BAD
DIRTY BUTTERFLY
RANDOM
STONING MARY
TRADE & GENERATIONS
TRUTH AND RECONCILIATION

Chris Hannan
ELIZABETH GORDON QUINN
SHINING SOULS

Liz Lochhead
BLOOD AND ICE
DRACULA *after* Stoker
EDUCATING AGNES ('The School
    for Wives') *after* Molière
GOOD THINGS
MARY QUEEN OF SCOTS GOT
    HER HEAD CHOPPED OFF
MEDEA *after* Euripides
MISERYGUTS ('The Miser')
    & TARTUFFE *after* Molière
PERFECT DAYS
THEBANS *after* Euripides & Sophocles

Linda McLean
ANY GIVEN DAY
ONE GOOD BEATING
RIDDANCE
SHIMMER
STRANGERS, BABIES

Joanna Murray-Smith
BOMBSHELLS
THE FEMALE OF THE SPECIES
HONOUR

Rona Munro
THE HOUSE OF BERNARDA ALBA
    after Lorca
THE INDIAN BOY
IRON
THE LAST WITCH
LITTLE EAGLES
LONG TIME DEAD
THE MAIDEN STONE
MARY BARTON *after* Gaskell
PANDAS
STRAWBERRIES IN JANUARY
    from de la Chenelière
YOUR TURN TO CLEAN THE STAIR
    & FUGUE

Chris Hannan

THE GOD
OF SOHO

NICK HERN BOOKS
London
www.nickhernbooks.co.uk

A Nick Hern Book

The God of Soho first published in Great Britain as a paperback original in 2011 by Nick Hern Books Limited, 14 Larden Road, London W3 7ST

The God of Soho copyright © 2011 Chris Hannan

Chris Hannan has asserted his right to be identified as the author of this work

Cover image: Small Back Room
Cover design: Ned Hoste, 2H

Typeset by Nick Hern Books, London
Printed in Great Britain by CLE Print Ltd, St Ives, Cambs PE27 3LE

A CIP catalogue record for this book is available from the British Library

ISBN 978 1 84842 168 4

The God of Soho was first performed at Shakespeare's Globe, London, on 27 August 2011, with the following cast:

JOE QUEENAN/TERRY CASH   Michael Camp
EDWARDO   Richard Clews
THE BIG GOD   Phil Daniels
MRS GOD   Miranda Foster
BAZ   Edward Hogg
THE NEW GOD   Will Mannering
NATTY   Emma Pierson
HANDMAIDEN/   Sarita Piotrowski
  HAIRY GODDESS
CLEM   Iris Roberts
STAN   Beatriz Romilly
TERESA   Jade Williams

MUSICIANS   King Porter Stomp

Director   Raz Shaw
Designer   Hannah Clark
Composer   Alex Silverman
Choreographer   Ann Yee

Author's Note

In the early stages of writing *The God of Soho* I had the
opportunity to work with the postgraduate students of the MA
Classical and Contemporary Text, Acting/Directing Course at
the RSAMD, Glasgow. In a series of workshops they helped me
to develop my ideas and gave a public performance of the first
draft.

I'm grateful for their creativity and support and would like to
dedicate the completed play to the nine postgraduates involved:

Victoria Beesley, Vanessa Coffey, Kathleen Culler, Euan
Cuthbertson, Eve Everette, Stephanie Falls, Ed McGurn, Gavin
Purdie and Stasi Schaeffer (director).

Chris Hannan

Characters

THE BIG GOD
SHIT GOD
THE DOG GODDESS
THE NO SHIT GOD
HANDMAIDEN
CLEM
THE NEW GOD
BAZ HAMMER
JOE QUEENAN
POLICEMAN
POLICEWOMAN
GROUCHO CLUB STAFF MEMBER
NATTY
STAN
EDWARDO
MRS GOD
HAIRY GODDESS
TERESA
TONY GOLDILOCKS
TERRY CASH
SECURITY WOMAN

Plus SEX WORKERS, FETISHISTS, PUNTERS, PEOPLE
FROM THE UNDERWORLD, MEDIA TYPES

This text went to press before the end of rehearsals and so may differ slightly from the play as performed.

ACT ONE

Scene One

Heaven. A convention of the GODS. *The* BIG GOD *enters.*

THE BIG GOD. The state of things in heaven and on the earth. And the reasons why. An inquiry. The evidence, weighing it sifting judging. Who's the crisis, that's the question. Who's the crisis and how did it begin? Can we agree on that?

SHIT GOD. Yes, big god.

THE DOG GODDESS (*played by a man*). Yes, god.

THE NO SHIT GOD. Yes, big god.

THE BIG GOD. There's a lack of loveliness in the world. There's a mood. It's like a giant rubbling around the cities of heaven and earth, crushing shops and cathedrals and stadiums beneath its feet as it

He smiles while he searches the debris of his mind for the word.

searches for something lovely, having not the smallest idea what loveliness looks like.

That's the situation. Who wants to start?

SHIT GOD. Before we begin; two of the gods are missing. Your daughter the goddess of love; and the new god.

THE BIG GOD. Yes; someone go and get the new god.

SHIT GOD. And your daughter?

THE BIG GOD. She's an Afghanistan of love. Ferocious, beautiful, unbeatable, best left in peace.

SHIT GOD. She keeps to her bed since that new god ditched her.

THE NO SHIT GOD. She hasn't changed the sheets since. She's very low. When she does drag herself out she circles around the garden like a water-logged rowing boat.

SHIT GOD. There's a theory that she's the one who's causing the problem.

THE BIG GOD. You, shit god, go and tell my daughter the gods want her to give an account of herself.

The SHIT GOD *exits.*

DOG GODDESS. Apparently she's lost her looks. (*Lapdog in her arms.*) I never wished her harm. I feel nothing but sympathy. The pain of losing one's looks, let me tell you, ugly people can count themselves lucky. To have been beautiful once, and then to discover all of a sudden that one's a dog – just hideous.

THE BIG GOD. I wouldn't say you're a dog.

DOG GODDESS. I wasn't talking about me.

CLEM *enters, pushed on in her bed. The bed has seen the goddess of love and sex and beauty in all her glory and witnessed her triumphs. It might also suggest her recent crushing defeat.*

I'm hoping nobody speaks for a while. I want to savour her beauty in silence.

THE BIG GOD. Say something unforgettable.

DOG GODDESS. She makes me vomit so she does.

THE BIG GOD. The poetry pours out of him.

DOG GODDESS. She really makes me spew. (*To* CLEM.) The more I look at you the lovelier you become. No wonder we all adore and worship you.

HANDMAIDEN. When she walks into a room peace breaks out.

DOG GODDESS. When you cry we go into mourning. Remember the time you paid me a royal visit. I laid on a very simple breakfast. A plain buttery roll with raspberry jam of a rare vintage and exquisite poise, which she took a few small bites out of and didn't finish. I was devastated. I thought, is the jam not of the stature I was led to believe; is the roll *too* ordinary. And for those few minutes she was with me, nothing in my life seemed trivial.

I bet you never imagine you might go bald.

CLEM. No, darling, I don't.

DOG GODDESS. Are you ever anxious when you're naked?

CLEM. No. I'm like the the bare-naked moon.

DOG GODDESS. You spend your nights alone.

CLEM. I'm wrapped in majesty.

The NEW GOD *enters in the background.*

THE BIG GOD. This new god. Can anyone explain him? As far as I can see he's got no regard for anything. He treats the rest of us gods with complete contempt. What's he the god of, atheism?

DOG GODDESS. Was he good in bed?

CLEM. He made me feel as juicy as a plum. Ever disturbed a wasp that's got sozzled inside a damson and then snoozed...

THE NEW GOD. Look at the goddess of love. Marooned on her bed.

THE BIG GOD. You spent all summer in that bed. It's hard to imagine why you would leave it, barring some unpleasant injury.

THE NEW GOD. Can we be quick about this.

THE BIG GOD. The state of things in heaven and on earth. Who's the crisis? What will make it better?

CLEM. You don't want to hear the whole unedifying story. We've nothing to be proud of, either of us. I never want to see him again; but I'd be prepared to forgive him with a kiss and forget all about it.

THE NEW GOD. Here?

CLEM. Don't be afraid, waspy. You won't drown. I promise not to try.

THE NEW GOD. You think I won't be able to stop?

You repel me.

THE BIG GOD. She's the goddess of love and sex and beauty.

THE NEW GOD. Nothing I can do about that.

THE BIG GOD. She was made from the beauty pouring out of a fucking fountain of beauty.

THE NEW GOD. After a while I dressed her up in certain items to make her more palatable. I study the grammar of desire, to me that's its drama and we liked, we both liked, she said she liked, we tried different things both liked certain items. The obviousness of them, the way some very florid flowers have markings for bees, as loud as the landing strip of an airport guiding them in. And don't say, but those markings are natural and certain items are not. You think human breasts are 'natural' look at apes, you see the same aesthetic? Desire has got its punctuation, its exclamation marks, its erotikons, it's a system of signs and we were playing with that. Then one night, suddenly accuses me of sex in the mind.

CLEM. I'd rather you.

THE NEW GOD. Suddenly this intellectual dishonesty. Sex *is* in the mind, *where else can it be*? So I left her and went, somewhere else, met someone, tried different things, and we liked we both liked, we tried various things both liked certain items. And interestingly she's fat, could be called unattractive some people would, but the you could call unattractive plus certain items equation is, interesting. The fact that certain items can abolish annihilate the inequality the fundamental inequality of good looks in some kind of radical erasure of difference.

CLEM. Someone set fire to me, I'm cold. I, my punctuation's in all the wrong places. Me naked didn't do anything for him. If I was naked he wasn't able to do it.

THE NEW GOD. Flesh.

CLEM. What's wrong with flesh?

THE NEW GOD. It's dull.

CLEM. You wanted my flesh badly enough when it was dressed to make it appetising. Your eyes were cold as a tile floor and afterwards you didn't talk you didn't speak.

THE NEW GOD. Don't flatter yourself it was you I wanted. You were a part of the equation.

CLEM. Which part of me was part of the equation?

THE NEW GOD. The part I didn't like.

CLEM (*putting it together*). The part of me you didn't like, plus certain items?

THE NEW GOD. And after all that, after I Picasso'd beauty and reconfigured its body and face in fresh new ways, you thought – just then – I was going to I dunno drown in the oblivion of your kiss. You wanted me back.

CLEM. Yes. You've stripped me of my skin, take me back. You're wearing my pride, take me back. You junkied up my blood, take me back. You make me feel bald, take me back. You stole with your words, you lied with your kisses, I want to spit out my tongue, please take me back I'll be better this time.

She means both parts of these broken-backed sentences – both the furious statements of what he's done to her, followed by the naked appeal of 'take me back'. The effect of this should almost be embarrassing – for the goddess of love to be so desperate and in public.

THE BIG GOD. And this is the goddess of love and sex and beauty.

Whatever it was you had has

posh poetic word for gone

fucking gone. He broke into the tabernacle of your

blank

and stole the contents. You've no power over anyone no more relationship with the world than a broken compass. Go to earth, start again, see what you can learn from them. It's an interesting thing about evolution – once something becomes extinct it never reappears. A species, a language. I mention that because you can die from now on.

The NEW GOD *exits.*

CLEM. There's nothing for me here.

THE NO SHIT GOD. Could she ever return?

THE BIG GOD. Could you ever forgive him?

CLEM. *Me* forgive *him*? No.

THE BIG GOD. You can't come back unless you forgive him. That's the law I'm afraid.

The BIG GOD *exits. The other* GODS *strip her of anything valuable and exit. All go except* CLEM *and the* DOG GODDESS.

CLEM. Have you any idea what the world is like?

DOG GODDESS. I wouldn't worry about it if I were you. You'll be dead before you know it.

CLEM. *Death.* Isn't that the sexiest dirtiest word you've ever heard?

DOG GODDESS. I prefer the word *lick*.

CLEM. What worries me is I don't have a character. I have a body that wants things and doesn't know how to get them. I don't know how it works. It's like discovering you're the wrong sex, do you get used to it?

DOG GODDESS. How would I know, dearie.

CLEM. No. I wasn't asking you, dog goddess. I was just
flinging out a question.

The DOG GODDESS *puts a sheet or blanket around her.*

DOG GODDESS. Where in the world will you go?

CLEM. I'll look for something sexier than sex.

DOG GODDESS. I wish I could come. You'll need someone
with some common sense. I often wonder who I get it from.
My own parents were insane believe it or not; and so were
their parents and their parents' parents.

CLEM. So you're some kind of bizarre freak?

DOG GODDESS. I suppose in a funny way I am. Now
remember me wherever you go and tell people how I stood
up for you and never let you go.

But that's a fib. The DOG GODDESS *didn't stand up for her.*

CLEM. I will.

*She exits, with music, through the groundlings in the yard. As
she steps down into them it's like being baptised in people or
in death.*

DOG GODDESS. What would it be like, where she's going, if
you had no looks, no knowledge, no wit, nothing to help you
along the way. I picture an addict. I see her holding out her
arms to beg, trying not to notice she has the least appealing
arms in the world.

She exits.

Scene Two

Soho. A rooftop. Night. Up through the trap onto the roof of the Groucho Club come BAZ HAMMER, *a rock musician, and a film actor called* JOE QUEENAN. BAZ *is holding a mirror with lines of coke already cut. Each thinks he's a bit more famous than the other.*

BAZ. woooo! roof of the insane, roof of the the Groucho the Groucho Club, king of the nuts drunk stars

JOE QUEENAN. those people people breaking through the bedroom door with axes, breaking through the bedroom door

BAZ. only the boss nutters have climbed out onto the roof of the Groucho Club only the über nutters

JOE QUEENAN. because as an actor i am trying to figure out what i'm doing here. and after three days of hoovering cocaina up my nose, what i need to know as an actor is – i mean this is the Groucho Club, yeah? – and there are people breaking through my bedroom door with axes!!!??? – so what i'm asking is, the people breaking through the door with axes are they people breaking through the door with axes

BAZ. yes

JOE QUEENAN. and i know that?

BAZ. yes

JOE QUEENAN. should i be concerned?

> BAZ *does a line.*

BAZ. that depends yeah on whether you're afraid of death

JOE QUEENAN. as an actor?

BAZ. as an arsehole.

JOE QUEENAN. after three days of doing charlie then possible
this is para para paranoia. you're let's face it you're Baz
Hammer, lead guitarist of *The Panic Attacks*

BAZ. paranoia then why are they breaking through the bedroom
door with axes

JOE QUEENAN. because you boarded up the door!

BAZ. it's the bag

JOE QUEENAN. bag?

BAZ. it's the bag man bag's fault

BAZ. who's down there in the club tonight, Sienna or Keira or
Liam or some film producers yeah, big-dick comedians
taking up a lot of room outstanding-ish artists that can give
you give you something worth fifty fifty k to hang on your
wall; the kind a rock stars people take their grandchildren to
see and a kennelful of intellectual louts and neds barking the
night away. everyone glowing in the famousness like it's the
Turkish baths. demigods, yes, but this bag yeah has seen
party nights where the gods of this world rioted their tits off
way up Mount fucking Heaven while lightning photographed
the mountain darkness; and the big gods of this earth
applauded the lightning, like it was cool yeah but not as big
as big a deal as them

JOE QUEENAN. so it's like the fashion accessory of the film
gods, worth what

BAZ. thirteen fourteen thousand? the fewness of those bags are
numbered in the hundreds more tigers on the earth than bags
like that

JOE QUEENAN. did you steal it?

BAZ. it's the girlfriend's

we're tearing each other up in the tabloids slash home. front
pages totally nuts man.

Axe noises.

JOE QUEENAN.... shitty shitty fuck fuck. she's sent men to kill us because of a handbag?

BAZ. it's the stuff in the bag. our fetish items. i give that sex shame scandal to the tabloids we will need to leave the country, and that is the decision i've been trying not to make the last couple days.

JOE QUEENAN. you're gonna rat yourself out to the tabloids?

BAZ. she's going to have a baby. i thought if she saw that stuff in the tabloids she might realise that beating the shit out of each other is suboptimal

it's a prison sentence being in love with that babe. she's my soulmate. sadly her soul is shut up inside the soul of a big bad nasty prison warder.

The axe noises have been persistent but now we hear the axe break through.

JOE QUEENAN. listen to them smashing down the door *they are in the room* and they are going to come up onto the roof with an axe with minimum an axe and what i resent is, where's my fucking exit? where do i go? you want me to just stand here and wait for them like a banana without any fucking dialogue. i am a fucking star man, my agent would not let me read this shit.

Up onto the roof come a POLICEMAN *and* POLICEWOMAN *with torches and a* MEMBER OF GROUCHO CLUB STAFF.

STAFF MEMBER/POLICEWOMAN. Where are you?

JOE QUEENAN (*hands in air*). He's there, he's fucking there, I'm Joe Queenan Joe Queenan Joe Queenan.

POLICEWOMAN (*suddenly recognising the star and falling under his spell*). Joe Queenan!

BAZ. He's been tipped as the next James Bond.

POLICEWOMAN (*genuine*). Yeah, you'd be perfect as James Bond.

STAFF MEMBER. Can I get you a sandwich, Mr Queenan?

JOE QUEENAN. No fine thanks.

STAFF MEMBER. Something from the bar?

BAZ. We're cool, man. It's nuts up here.

STAFF MEMBER. You a club member, sir?

BAZ. Me?

STAFF MEMBER. Yes.

BAZ. No.

STAFF MEMBER. Then can I ask you to leave?

They are waiting for him to go.

BAZ. Ever been on the front pages, Joe...

JOE QUEENAN. No.

BAZ....the front pages is like the cameras are rolling you make
a mistake they don't chop it out in the edit. The mistake is
what the paparazzi are there for, all you can hear is the
panicky stutter of a thousand machine-gun flashes gunning
you down. It's not the movies, Joe: blood gets spilled...

BAZ *exits.*

POLICEWOMAN. Right, let's get down off this roof. Listen,
Joe, this is really naff, but could you sign your autograph for
me?

JOE QUEENAN. Sure. Sure, no problem.

POLICEWOMAN. Thanks, man. I'd be really grateful. My dad
thinks you're gorgeous.

They exit.

Scene Three

NATTY*'s house. She is carried or pushed onstage, still in her nightclothes. Where the goddess of love entered in a bed, NATTY enters on a large white-leather sofa. Outsize. It's a his-and-hers sofa. She's perched with her feet on the seat and her bum on the back. One half of the sofa has a drawing of NATTY etched on it with 'NATTY' written above the drawing; the other half has BAZ with 'BAZ' written above it. It's a piece they've commissioned.*

NATTY *is trying to burn off a tattoo and yelling in pain. STAN enters, NATTY's celebrity publicist. STAN earns maybe half a million a year and dresses accordingly.*

STAN. Natty.

NATTY. A thousand times a day I say to myself, Natty, you are a wanker, you are a shallow deceitful wanker. If you could stop thinking about youself for a single second, you selfish self-centered shallow tit of a wanker, you might be able to breathe. I'd cut myself if it wasn't such a cliché. Any ugly sub-fat teenage girl can cut herself, that shit is all rinsed out. Please, God, tell me some new way to hurt myself cos I am loathsome.

NATTY *gets up off the sofa. This reveals that someone has added 'TARD' to the end of 'BAZ', in rather a home-made fashion.*

STAN. You're not loathsome.

NATTY. As my publicist how would you describe me?

STAN *can look you in the face and text at the same time.*

STAN. You don't know yourself, Natty. You can be quite nice sometimes.

NATTY. I am not nice, Stan. I'm a nasty bad screw-face girl and I got a nasty bad rottweiler mind that is vex with me twenty-four-seven. Can I come to bed with you?

STAN. Course you can, sweetness.

NATTY. I like it when someone's made the sheets warm.

STAN. That's why I'm here, doll.

NATTY. I've lost my man, Stan. I can't keep nothing down. He's my lining. Nothing I wear looks good neither. Why'd he leave me, Stan?

STAN. You beat in his face, babes.

NATTY. I melted his fucking nose.

STAN. You kicked him in the plums.

NATTY. And now I've gone and done worser than that. I hired a bad man to scare the shit out of him with a shooter. I didn't ask your advice cos I knew what you'd say.

STAN. You could go to prison for that.

NATTY. Point of view of being my publicist d'you think I've made a mistake?

STAN. Point of view of being your publicist I'd *like* you to go to prison, sweets. But as your human friend I don't think you'd learn nothing from it.

NATTY. He left me no choice, Stan. He jacked my 1950s Hermès Kelly bag. You know how much I love that bag.

STAN. It's iconic.

NATTY. It's got that dead-princess look. It's so feminine and so sad.

STAN. And so you.

NATTY. And Baz put a lot of private things in the bag. Sex things.

STAN. What kind of sex things?

NATTY. Obscure shit. Painful things.

STAN. So you hired a man with a shooter?

NATTY. I told them exactly what to do, Stan. I said they was to be proportional. I said Death no. Terror yes. The money I am giving em I want a bag of terror. While I got all of that to think about can you do the funeral arrangements?

STAN. For who?

NATTY. For my mum you yo-yo. St Christopher's phoned last night. I want to bring the body here, Stan. Is it strange to have your dead mum in your house?

STAN. A corpse is a bit of a stranger. You keep expecting them to do something and they don't.

NATTY. That was the worst thing I hated about mum's cancer; she knew everybody was watching her. She didn't have nowhere to hide the pain. It was hard for the horrible cow; I'll give her a big state funeral in Sacred Heart Church, Camberwell.

They exit.

Scene Four

Out of the underworld – SEX WORKERS, FETISHISTS, PUNTERS, *maybe a* DOMINATRIX *from a whip club,* DOG PEOPLE *in collars and their* OWNERS, PEOPLE *in chains and handcuffs, and* MEDIA TYPES.

A song – 'Sexier Than Sex'

UNDERWORLD PEOPLE (*singing*).
    Fuck you
    Fuck you over we will fuck you
    Fuck you
    Fuck you over we will fuck you

Fuck you
Fuck you over we will fuck you
Fuck you
Fuck you over we will fuck you

CLEM, *the former goddess of love, descends from the heavens.*

Over the UNDERWORLD PEOPLE *she sings.*

CLEM (*singing*).
Oh I'm as sore as a King's Cross whore
Looking for more
And more and more and more
Searching for more

UNDERWORLD PEOPLE (*singing*).
Fuck you
Fuck you over we will fuck you
Fuck you
Fuck you over we will fuck you
Fuck you
Fuck you over we will fuck you
Fuck you
Fuck you over we will fuck you

CLEM *reaches the earth.*

PIMP (*singing*).
Hey there
What you doing here in King's Cross
Hangin
Like a kid with all her things lost

CLEM (*singing*).
Looking
Feel it in my solar plexus
Wanting
Something sexier than sex is

PROSTITUTE. What's she want?

PIMP. Something sexier than sex.

PROSTITUTE. Sleep.

MEDIA PERSON. I tell you what's sexier than sex. Fame.

They sing.

> Sex is
> Something that you do in private
> Fame's more
> You go out in your Jag and drive it
> Stopping
> Only when the Jag arrives at
> Somewhere
> They will love you all day long

FETISHIST. I'll tell you what's sexier than sex. Pain.

CLEM. Pain?

FETISHIST (*singing*).
> Pain is
> Pain is sexier than sex is
> Tied with
> Gaffa and electric flexes;
> Straight sex
> Don't do nothing for us
> Ssgone yeah
> Like tyrannosaurus rexes

CLEM (*singing*).
> Oh I'm as sore as a King's Cross whore
> Looking for more
> And more and more and more
> Searching for more

While simultaneously:

UNDERWORLD PEOPLE (*singing*).
> Fuck you
> Fuck you over we will fuck you
> Fuck you
> Fuck you over we will fuck you
> Fuck you

> Fuck you over we will fuck you
> Fuck you
> Fuck you over we will fuck you

PROSTITUTE. Listen; if anyone knows what's sexier than sex it's us.

THREE PROSTITUTES (*singing*).
> Sex is
> Boring boring boring boring
> Sex is
> Boring boring dull as Texas
> Sex is
> Boring boring boring boring
> Truss me

The PROSTITUTES *lift their skirts. Their knickers are stuffed with cash, back and front.*

> Cash is sexier than sex is

Everybody exits, leaving CLEM *and* EDWARDO.

They go on a walk around.

CLEM. Where are we now?

EDWARDO. This is Soho. Where you live before here?

CLEM. Nowhere.

EDWARDO. Yeah?

I'm bipolar by the way. Yeah. I'm schizophrenic too. Yeah. It's interesting. They section me for my own safety. You like do anything before you became homeless?

CLEM. No.

EDWARDO. Got any illnesses?

CLEM. No.

EDWARDO. No? You're not very interesting.

CLEM. I'm called Clem.

EDWARDO. Right. Do you mind if I call you Ward Two. You can sleep in my basement, Ward Two. We go to bed before the old queens and trannies head home from the pubs so it's nice being up a side street where you can hide from the negativity and the people who wanna pull you down to their level.

CLEM. What's the smell around here?

EDWARDO. You asking me a question?

CLEM. Yes.

EDWARDO. Ask it again and this time use my name.

CLEM. Edwardo, what's the smell around here?

EDWARDO. That's nicer.

CLEM. Some kind of thin. Doesn't cover anything.

EDWARDO. Yeah man, slike a blanket in jail.

CLEM. The smell of sex and money. Like you can get what you want if you have the cash.

Will you show me how to be a homeless person?

EDWARDO. I'm nothing like the rest of the rubbish. Go down and make your bed, I'll doss on the steps.

CLEM *goes down steps as though to a basement.*
EDWARDO *makes a bed on the steps.*

You hear people walking past all night. I just look down on them, man. Why they up so late? Always shouting like summing terrible has happened. You know what they are? Noise, man. Noises. I turn on my side and pull the blanket over me and I think what do they know? Some of us got to be up early and fucking thinking about things.

EDWARDO *lies down, goes to sleep.*

Scene Five

We can still see EDWARDO *on the steps down to the basement.*

But we are now in Heaven. Enter the BIG GOD *and* MRS GOD.

MRS GOD. Don't leave me on my own. Heaven is falling.

THE BIG GOD. It's not literally falling.

MRS GOD. Yes it is. It's literally falling.

THE BIG GOD. If it was literally falling we would be falling.

MRS GOD. I know.

THE BIG GOD. Well then. Talk sense.

MRS GOD. We are falling.

    The BIG GOD *considers this possibility. He is not very sure whether he is falling or not.*

THE BIG GOD. No. If we were falling we would know.

MRS GOD. It's like Clem was a pillar holding up the heavens and now that she's gone...

    As many other of the GODS *as possible enter. They push on a bed – once the bed of the goddess of love – but now stripped and bare.*

    The mattress is stained with the shape of a heart, smudged.

THE NO SHIT GOD (*with inner strength*). Sometimes people cannot see things for themselves. Sometimes people need things to be pointed out. Heaven is falling.

THE BIG GOD. It's not literally falling.

THE NO SHIT GOD. Yes. It is. It's literally falling. We are indistinguishable from each other. It's hard to separate one thought from another and do it for long enough to know if it really was a thought or not. It doesn't matter who is who. One minute I'll be her, the next I'm you.

The SHIT GOD *and the* HAIRY GODDESS *have identical orange or orang-utan-type hair.*

SHIT GOD. I hate it when I have her hair.

HAIRY GODDESS. I hate when I have her hair.

SHIT GOD. I don't like *my* hair either, but at least it's mine.

HAIRY GODDESS. You can keep it.

SHIT GOD. Her hair's like that all over. Her arms, her backside, her sporran.

THE NO SHIT GOD. Things were bad *before* you sent your daughter away but now…

SHIT GOD. The dog goddess has lost her mind.

THE BIG GOD. He was fragile at the best of times.

SHIT GOD. Now she's broken.

THE BIG GOD. Yes. I came across him sitting on that bed by the river. When he saw me he got up and stood on the bed –

The BIG GOD *stands on the bed.*

– and said, are you my father? Are you my father or the ghost of my father? I begged you not to send me away, with these very arms – and look – you chopped them off. Oh, I wish I was lovely. I said you are lovely. He said I'm not. I'm a very highly strung chihuahua with neither wit nor talent.

Everyone is looking at the BIG GOD *like he has done something somewhere on a continuum between tactless and sacrilegious.*

MRS GOD. Will you come down from there? You're embarrassing everyone. You're standing on your daughter's bed.

THE BIG GOD. I'm showing you what he did.

MRS GOD. You're impersonating someone who's mentally afflicted.

THE NO SHIT GOD. The other gods have asked me to speak with you. Sometimes people cannot see things for themselves. Maybe it's time you stood aside.

THE BIG GOD. You don't imagine anyone else could god this black-mind solitude. There are black holes inside here – (*Indicates his mind.*) busy uncreating everything, places of utter darkness, and I am not afraid because I *am* those fucking places. I could god this universe with *half* a bastarding brain. You want me to bring my daughter back, is that it?

THE NO SHIT GOD. Yes.

THE BIG GOD. It's done. I will eat this problem and shit it. Go on, get lost, you're mad as a sheep, you are; and have the decency to wear an expression on your face, one of you, it's enough to put me off my food.

The GODS *exit, leaving only the* BIG GOD *and his wife.*

MRS GOD. People used to worship me of course. I was the goddess of everything. Fields. Battles. Childbirth. They brought me honey sorrows brides lambs and things from the sea. I had everything. Three pairs of tits, the adoration of the world, you. I'm still very – I wouldn't say I was happy, no, I wouldn't say that – but content, yes, certainly. I've had my insides removed, life is good.

She has an outside bowel. It's in the shape of a heart and she carries it rather like a clutch bag.

THE BIG GOD. Does that thing have to be transparent?

MRS GOD. It's postmodern.

THE BIG GOD. I see.

MRS GOD. I don't want to be stereotyped as the typical wife of an enormously powerful male. I mean, yes, I'm enthusiastic; (*The bag froths with shit.*) bubbly; (*The bag bubbles.*) I've kept my looks. But I like to think I'm also challenging. (*Bag bubbles.*) Is that the reason you find me difficult to be with?

THE BIG GOD. That's one reason.

MRS GOD. Am I too open?

THE BIG GOD. You're doing the toilet.

MRS GOD. What?

THE BIG GOD. You're doing business.

MRS GOD. Don't know where that comes from, I eat once a month if that.

THE BIG GOD. That's the shit you talk.

MRS GOD. Are you going to find Clem? I'll come with you if you like.

THE BIG GOD. Awww.

MRS GOD. Would you like that?

THE BIG GOD. Do you promise to stop (missing continuous tense) do you promise to stop continuous-tense shitting? I'm constipated for goodness' sake. I haven't shat in a thousand years. Are you doing that on purpose to annoy me?

MRS GOD. You're not going to get very far without me.

THE BIG GOD (*enraged even to tears*). Yes you can come. No doubt you've been put in my path to teach me some kind of lesson.

He exits, she follows.

Scene Six

We can still see EDWARDO *sleeping on the steps down to the basement, but we are now in Soho because one or two Soho types walk by, including a* PROSTITUTE *still looking for customers after a long night. She scooshes some deodorant up her top and down her knickers, then exits when a* CUSTOMER *shows up.*

The NEW GOD *enters.*

THE NEW GOD. The bag with the fetish items. He could have dumped it anywhere but by a strange coincidence –

He smiles.

– he dumped it in that basement. So when Clem wakes up and opens the bag she's down there clutching in her sleep, she will go on a journey like being on a very bad trip in a very bad part of town.

He looks down into the basement.

She's sleeping with a dog. Oh, she looks quite appealing there.

He goes down into the basement. When he re-emerges he has undergone a profound change.

He comes up the steps backwards, followed by CLEM *holding the Hermès Kelly bag.*

How come I never before. World-shatteringly beautiful she is. Till my world shattered?

I'm jealous of a dog. She had her hand on his ribs and they both looked so serious together.

You know the way you breathe sometimes, when you're afraid you're, going to vomit, deep breaths but careful. Seeing her sleeping on a pavement, seeing how hard she is, how tough, how much she can take, and how fragile, how easily she could die, and all my feelings have been ungagged. I guess I was too much for Pride to swallow so he's spewed me up, stinking of my own shame and smeared with (   ).

CLEM *has knelt down somewhere with the bag.*

CLEM. Edwardo, i woke up and this was beside me

EDWARDO. fucking meteorite bag man

CLEM. like someone wants rid of it

EDWARDO. could be the four horsemen of the apocalypse in there. Death, Terror, Shit and Bewilderment.

CLEM. what' ll I do with it?

EDWARDO. open it, man. madness been shut up for too long.

She opens the bag. Music. Like a choir of angels singing twisted lyrics; or like the divine gone mad. CLEM *looks at the inside of the bag.*

CLEM. are they instruments?

medical instruments?

someone's equipment.

She gets up, walks away, slowly. She's perplexed out of her skin.

it's like the apparatus of a smile.

someone's made, someone's gone to a lot of trouble

the details. and someone has manufactured someone owns a small manufactory which produces

the apparatus employed to achieve a smile.

is it a doctor's bag not a doctor's bag the opposite of a doctor's bag, is it the opposite of a doctor's bag? someone who steals your skin?

EDWARDO *has found a photograph in there of* NATTY *dressed in the gear or performing acts. He holds it out but* CLEM *doesn't come to look at it.*

EDWARDO. this is her. this is her using the equipment.

CLEM (*not coming anywhere near*). i see.

EDWARDO. it's her sex things. you would be *mad* rich you took this to the papers. she's famous. funny thing is, she's got a sister thass homeless innit.

CLEM. she's got a sister?

EDWARDO. lives in a hostel near here, drinks superlager churchyard of St Fridays any day she's got the money.

CLEM. we got to give this back to someone. can we go to the churchyard of St Fry's?

EDWARDO. best not go near Teresa. she is mental.

CLEM. how mental exactly? more mental than you?

EDWARDO. no. no way, man. i am bipolar, schizophrenic and i got agoraphobia, which is the Rolls fucking Royce of mental illnesses when you're homeless, yeah. i am mental hospital celebrity mental. but what keeps me in good stead through my sufferings is my steadiness. i'm comfortable with my illnesses. Teresa? Teresa is the last refuge of Teresa. the tabloids will treat us politer than Teresa.

CLEM. i want to compare you with Teresa.

She exits, EDWARDO *follows her with the bag.*

THE NEW GOD. What's different about her? It's like her body has woken up. It has some knowledge I don't have. In the basement I noticed she had a sort of purplish rash, here where her face was lying on a crack in the paving; I wanted to be in the same world as her so I could dab it with cotton wool and wince in sympathy.

Could I do that? Could I become a man? I might drown in the terror. I might choke on the anonymity. I might sink like you. In the history of the universe was that the first emotion – fear? If that were the case why would I even consider entering the world of the slug and the lettuce and why would my heart be headbutting my chest. Maybe there was an emotion which preceded fear. The desire to learn. To investigate. To discover.

Exits through the groundlings in the yard, like being baptised in people or in death. With music – evocative of a solemn excitement.

Scene Seven

The BIG GOD *and* MRS GOD *enter, taller and larger than life.*
They are wearing the same outfits as before, but everything
bigger. They look like extended slightly cartoonish versions of
themselves. MRS GOD*'s external bowel is scaled up.*

MRS GOD. It's exhausting. The isolation. You talk to people
they don't hear you.

THE BIG GOD (*a thought strikes him*). I tell you what's
exhausting. The isolation. You talk to people they don't hear
you.

MRS GOD. It's like I don't exist.

THE BIG GOD (*new-minted thought*). It's like I don't exist.

MRS GOD. What went wrong with us? You used to find me
attractive. I was your (*Her bag shits.*) treasure. I was your
(*Shit.*) flower. You said I had nipples like champagne corks.
You dined on my breasts. Oh the years, the years. I tried.
Look what I did to myself. Look how I beautified myself.
And for what? You always thought there was someone more
wonderful (*Shit.*) more (*Shit.*) glamorous. Well, where is she?

In a fire-blackened tower block in Tottenham I heard a
woman cry last night. She was bald. Her husband had left
her with four kids. It was three in the morning and the crying
was so feeble, that was the terrifying part; like she was
frightened the neighbours would tell her to shut it she wasn't
pretty enough to be pitied.

THE BIG GOD. Yes. That's *very* sad.

Below them EDWARDO, TERESA *and* CLEM *enter,*
TERESA *goes behind a pillar to examine the contents of the*
bag.

MRS GOD. Here's Clem now – Oh, how much you love your children when you see them at a distance!

THE BIG GOD. Is she dead? Is that the ghost of Clem?

MRS GOD. No.

THE BIG GOD. Why can't she hear us? Why can't she see us?

EDWARDO *and* TERESA *exit.*

CLEM *hangs back.*

MRS GOD. Oh Clem, I don't know which of us is more alone, you or me.

She drops petals on CLEM*'s head, like an expression of love or to mark her inability to be present.*

CLEM *exits.*

THE BIG GOD. You know when there's tears way down at the roots of your eyes. Your eyes are dry but you know the tears are down there hiding in the dark below the cellars. Look, would you do me a favour? Would you go and find my wife?

MRS GOD. I am your wife.

He exits, she follows.

Scene Eight

Inside NATTY*'s house.* NATTY *enters, getting into a dress.*

NATTY. Stan! Stan!

STAN *enters.*

Stan, Baz is coming. I was in the garden, man, I could hear them. The paps. They are all over this tonight. Shouting at him. Shouting orders. Then when he does what they say? Nothing but cameras going off. Kisskisskissskisskisskisskiss. Kissing every piece of him, man. Kissing his nipples.

STAN. We got this charity gig for the limbless tonight, remember. If you beat in his face there are a hundred snappers waiting to splat that pic all over the papers tomorrow morning like a piece of roadkill, Natty, and nothing about the limbless.

NATTY. I love the limbless.

STAN. If you lose your temper

NATTY. I won't lose my temper

STAN. You always lose your temper.

NATTY. Stan, I ain't going to waste my temper on that waste man. What are my tits saying?

STAN. Tit is not one of my languages.

NATTY. I want them very much in the background but still there, like a possible future that I'm too sad to even think about right now.

BAZ enters.

BAZ. look, i cannot overemphasise enough the lastness of things

NATTY. death

BAZ. if we're going for the maximum

NATTY. death. don't want the funeral to be nothing bout me. let her be the star for once in her life. i'm sorry, i get emotional about this.

She pauses to be emotional.

why do we always have to grab

BAZ. need

NATTY. grab

BAZ. need

NATTY. grab grab grab. where's my bag?

BAZ. bag?

NATTY. bag

BAZ. dumped it

NATTY. you what it?

BAZ. man was after me, I got shit of it. dumped it on the streets

NATTY. i got to give you the kudos of coming here and saying that. you took private things belongs to me and emptied them out over the streets like a bin man or summing

BAZ. this unknown man was impending my death yeah

NATTY. like bin man or summing

NATTY *moves away, to change the point of attack.*

tell ya I got a new dealer?

BAZ. yeah?

NATTY. yeah. Shed.

BAZ. Shed yeah

NATTY. we was sparkin up and chattin shit, me and Shed yeah. he says a dealer does not attract a nice type of girlfriend, most of the girls a dealer attracts they don't want your dick inside them except it's dipped in coke. and once you got a girlfriend he says you cannot get shit of her. he says you so much as thinks about getting shit of her she clocks it

BAZ. yeah

NATTY. you could be driving and she could be sittin beside you and she clocks it and lets loose the dogs of her mouth upon you and she can't don't even know how to stop them till you crash the fucking car. then she supposes you crash the car on purpose and that's it, she starts to conjure how to put you in prison

yeah. you overestimate people at your peril.

BAZ. nice. you rehearse that speech? yes, no, nice, interesting use of, comparison between me and a drug dealer's bitch, *unstated* comparison. class.

NATTY. you acted like you was my lover but you was juss a thief biding his time.

BAZ....i ain't a thief

NATTY. you was going to sell me to the tabloids, bitch.

BAZ. you built a bonfire of all my gear that front-paged in three papers. you burned the bed my pride my Xbox. after you do that, how can i come back here in full view of my fan base. then thanks be to God your mum dies and that's a window of opportunity to rock up and offer you consolation. but it's only a small chance. the paps await. the fan has shit the ceiling. you throw me out tonight, you make me look bad tonight, I cannot come back again in a fucking disguise. i'm gasping. my heart is going epileptic. iss like a fish on the deck of a boat

NATTY. floundering.

BAZ. floundering, man.

NATTY. never even liked sex before you. was like doing a scratchcard, thass exact. you do it and when you don't win iss annoyin; it's like why'd I imagine I was going to win this time. then they was you. it was heaven in your arms. i never came till you come along. yeah. grim. didn't never come till you showed me the way

then you go and give it all away. leave it on the streets of Soho.

STAN *enters, followed shortly afterwards by* TERESA, CLEM *and* EDWARDO.

STAN. You got some visitors, Natty. It's your sister Teresa.

TERESA. She knows I'm her sister. I heard about Mum.

NATTY. Did you hear about Mum, yeah?

TERESA. Yeah. It was in the papers.

NATTY. D'you like my house though?

TERESA. It's mock-Tudor? Is it a copy of summing?

NATTY. It's not a copy, Teresa. Every little thing you see is an authentic reproduction. Cept the white marble. That's real.

TERESA. Thass the only reason I'm here, case you was losing touch with reality. I got nothin material things but I got the streets and the realness.

NATTY. Thass important. I don't ever want to forget what's going on down on the ground. The day I forget that I'm finished, ss why the public love me. You're a good reminder you are I need reminders like you I should keep you as a reminder. The end of the day I'm just an ordinary person.

TERESA. I know that, Natty. You used to wet the bed of the bunk above me.

NATTY. The thing is I'm no different to Teresa is. I'm nothing just like she is.

TERESA. I got the sereneness. Thass the difference. The end of the day we're the same, only I got the spirituality of living on the streets.

NATTY. Iss the spiritual things in life that's important in life. (*Pointing to her ceiling.*) Thass the gods up there. All them gold bottoms. I said I want the gods done in gold or it won't be realistic.

TERESA. You take them pillars from a church?

NATTY. Your style is your personality, Teresa, you don't find it down the back of a sofa. I had to import them pillars from Italy.

TERESA. Someone in the Mafia send them? They got that blandiosity gangstas like.

NATTY. Mmmm. When you think about it your personality's the most expensive thing you got. Look at you for instance. It's cost you everything.

TERESA. She found your bag.

NATTY. You found my bag?

TERESA. Someone left it on the streets.

NATTY. A thief must of dropped it.

TERESA. It had these personality things in it.

NATTY. You look inside?

TERESA. We had to look inside or how'd we of known it was yours.

NATTY. You show all your homeless friends my sex shame?

NATTY goes to the discovery space and opens a door, holds it open, revealing an open coffin. Or perhaps a coffin on a bier is wheeled onto the stage

You can see Mum if you want. You wanna see Mum? I'm sure she'd like to see you, Teresa. She said that on her deathbed. She said she'd like to see you. She said it would be nice to see Teresa.

TERESA goes to see her mum in the coffin. You only ever see your mum in a coffin once and you are never so alone. You don't know what to do or how you'll react. But then you see your mum and what happens is none of your choosing.

TERESA. Oh Mummy!

What's wrong with her? She looks false. I'll do her make-up. Who left her looking like that.

BAZ. Are you okay, Teresa?

NATTY. Oh God I'm so shit.

BAZ. You're not shit.

NATTY. I am shit.

BAZ. You're not shit.

NATTY. I'm so shit.

BAZ. You are not shit.

NATTY. Piece. Of. Shit.

BAZ. Natty. You're not shit.

NATTY. I'm shit. Shit. Shit.

BAZ. You're not, Natty.

NATTY. I'm shitness.

BAZ. No Natty. You're not.

NATTY. I'm made of shit.

BAZ. You're not shit.

NATTY. I am. I'm so shit the queen should give me a shitehood.

BAZ. Don't keep saying you're shit, Natty.

NATTY. You're losing patience with me.

BAZ. I'm not.

NATTY. Can hear it in your voice.

BAZ. I'm not losing patience.

NATTY. I wish I was human.

BAZ. You are human.

NATTY. I'm not. I'm shit.

TERESA. Oh Jesus. Me me me, look at me. It don't make you some kind of heroine the fact you're shit. Do something about it.

NATTY. Are you saying I'm shit? Are you saying I'm fucking shit?

BAZ. She's not, Natty.

NATTY. She's calling me shit, she found her hair in a bin.

BAZ. I'm floundering, Natty. I'm dying.

NATTY. Can I have my bag please, Teresa?

TERESA. He's got it.

CLEM (*to* NATTY). You're amazing. Do you mind if I just touch you?

NATTY (*to* EDWARDO). Can I have my bag back?

EDWARDO. Can I have my bag back, Edwardo? (Chuff chuff.)

NATTY. Can I have my bag back, Edwardo? (Chuff chuff.)

EDWARDO. In the right context yeah I cannot speak highly enough of chives.

EDWARDO *exits*.

TERESA. He put it somewhere to keep it safe.

NATTY. You keeping it so you can look down on me, is that it?

BAZ. Natty, can you stop, man?

NATTY (*to* BAZ). Say another word and I will beat in your face, you get me? I've made excuse after excuse for ya but I'm wore out with your the way you act like I'm some huge ugly animal. Like I'm a big dog with sad saucer eyes that drools these thick ropes of spit. And you have to hug it and make out it's beautiful and keep it placated or it'll fucking die of sadness.

You best be gone before I go out tonight. I got to get all branded up for this charity gig.

BAZ. The snappers will gun me down I go now.

NATTY. Fucking die, mate. Stan, phone an architect, I want this house demolished.

BAZ. You know why it's impossible to have a conversation with you, because you always say the exact thing you don't want to say. Fuck it, I'm going to get twatted.

NATTY *has exited with* STAN. BAZ *exits the other way…*

TERESA. I'll go calm her down. I'll either talk some sense into her or give her Largactil.

TERESA *exits*.

CLEM. To be as naked as Natty. Raw-skinned butcher naked. She put on every piece of ugly she owned and showed it off like an Oscar frock. She's a goddess of ugly; fat bridesmaids in peach dresses with short puffy sleeves puffing up their puffy arms should worship her as their very own; couples in tracksuits and rosary beads should do honour to her. She's it. She's what I've been looking for.

EDWARDO *enters*.

EDWARDO. Where is the snapping crocodilic mass of rage.

CLEM. She's the model.

STAN *enters*.

STAN. Edwardo, can Natty speak to you about her bag?

EDWARDO. No.

STAN. She paid eighteen thousand when she bought it.

EDWARDO. Don't want money.

STAN. Can you tell us where you put it?

EDWARDO. Money ain't no use to me, mate. I got illnesses, you get me?

EDWARDO *exits*.

CLEM. Will you tell Natty I wish her all good things?

STAN. She don't know you, babes.

Scene Nine

The BIG GOD *and* MRS GOD *enter* NATTY*'s garden.*

THE BIG GOD. Fucking England. What school will we send the fucking children to? And class the class system what the fuck is class?

MRS GOD. The difference between me and you, dear.

THE BIG GOD. You being so posh you'd think you'd have an inside toilet.

MRS GOD. Smell that. A garden at night cooling down after all the hot and bother of the sun. Roses and the moistness of dirt. Roses try too hard. The dirt is the note that pulls at you and draws you back.

THE BIG GOD. In days gone by I'd have agreed with you right away, that's a rose I would have said. But nowadays I have to put it together. I see it flat, like I have a map of it, and then I model that in three dimensions, and that way I retrieve my memory of a rose. And then I can say I'm fairly certain – plus or minus – that something's a rose.

Yes, that's a rose. The roses that I *remember* had an unfuckable loveliness.

MRS GOD. So does this one. Look.

THE BIG GOD. I'm in the wrong fucking part of my brain. There's another hemisphere of the brain where they keep things away from me; the breath of the baby, the strength of gratitude, the character of the knife, the arrangement of the parts, the smack of the butter, the organisation of the brain, the unstoppability of the tears when you start sobbing, the reassurance of the end.

I know the other hemisphere is there but I can't reach it.

MRS GOD. How long has this been going on for?

THE BIG GOD. It's difficult to remember exactly.

MRS GOD. Were you like this when you told Clem to leave heaven?

THE BIG GOD. Oh yes. I'd say so, yes.

Up on the balcony the NEW GOD *enters in the persona of a wine salesman called* TONY GOLDILOCKS, *with bottles of wine and bottle opener.* TERRY CASH *the chef joins him, swirling glass of wine and sampling it.*

TERRY CASH (*a loud northerner*). You do not want to be a chef for a celebrity. What you want to be is a celebrity chef. I worked in a Michelin star restaurant before I came here to work for Natty. My signature dish was spicy ox tongue Korean style on a noodle coriander and cucumber salad. Tonight she ordered curry flavour Super Noodles on white bread and sent it back cos the bread weren't buttered right. Still she'll be a good anecdote in the future when I'm on the telly or that. She'll give my story a bit of madness. How long you been in the wholesale-wine game?

TONY GOLDILOCKS. All my life really.

He pours a wine.

Some wines command respect in any conversation. Nothing nicer if you're some rich barrister or some city bastard than unbuttoning your suit in a restaurant come seven o'clock, letting your belly relax after the stresses of the day and enjoying the name of a very fine wine as it unfolds on your palate. To be pissed is lovely; to be pissed and rich is charming; and to be knowledgeable about the wine that has transported you to the fields of joy is positively learnèd. Here, try this one.

MRS GOD. I suppose he knows Clem's here and he needed a way in.

THE BIG GOD. A wine salesman! Of all the ways to die.

TERRY CASH. The question I ask myself about a wine is. Do I want a lot lot more of it? I want a lot lot more of that. What did you say your name was?

TONY GOLDILOCKS. Tony. Tony Goldilocks.

TERRY CASH. Tony Goldilocks. That's unusual.

TONY GOLDILOCKS. Is it?

TERRY CASH. In real life yes.

TONY GOLDILOCKS. I really wouldn't know. I was brought up Orthodox Jewish, you see. There's a whole flock of Goldilocks in Finchley. Can I suggest twelve bottles of the red for the funeral and eighteen of this white?

TERRY CASH. I'll get my chequebook and some brandy. Natty's off to a charity gig for the limbless tonight. Those security gates open there'll be a feeding frenzy of snappers.

TERRY CASH *exits*.

BAZ *enters followed by* CLEM. BAZ *is leaving the house to face the press.*

BAZ. People always saying we live in a amoral universe. I wish we did. You ask me the universe is a hard bastard. You love someone the universe imposes a moral obligation to fucking love them. And if you don't know how or they don't know how or you can't work out how, the moral universe will crush you in its moral bastarding embrace.

Would be nice if the press snappers could get a piccy of that: the moral universe crushing me in its moral fucking embrace.

CLEM. she's amazing. i suppose when you get to know her as well as you do bet she's amazing but totally ordinary and that's what's amazing because in a way we're all amazing but totally ordinary… not that i'm comparing myself to her…

i think, to me character should have a personality of its own like wine or something and what she has is

it's amazing. She's got this amazing

Presence. like i dunno like a hugely expensive designer price tag

BAZ. or the absence of a price tag. the clothes that don't have a price tag. that's what you call presence

CLEM. or a princess who has so much presence she can nod to left and right and hand out her princessiness with a smile

BAZ. or a hissing fucking swan.

CLEM. when you're in the company of someone who has presence i expect even a breakfast is unforgettable.

He's not even looking at her.

BAZ. do i go out there and face the murdering hissing? or do i give her one more chance? oh fuck, i'll give her one more chance

He goes to exit.

CLEM. I love you, Baz. I mean I love Natty I love both of you. I suppose I'm like Natty in lots of ways. I'm shit too.

She's trying to be NATTY *or to out-*NATTY NATTY *in order to seduce him.*

BAZ. You're not shit.

CLEM. I am shit.

BAZ. You're not shit.

CLEM. I'm deeply shit.

BAZ. You're not shit.

CLEM. I'm more shit than Natty.

BAZ. You're not shit.

CLEM. I'm very shit.

BAZ. You're not.

CLEM. How shit do you want me to be?

BAZ. I'm going to have a word with Natty.

CLEM. Natty Natty Natty. Who even *is* she?

BAZ *exits*.

TONY GOLDILOCKS. Clem?

CLEM (*to* TONY GOLDILOCKS). Have you been eavesdropping?

MRS GOD. No!

THE BIG GOD. Not the kind of thing you want to see.

TONY GOLDILOCKS. It's me. Wait there till I come down.

CLEM. Don't come anywhere near me or I'll go.

TONY GOLDILOCKS. Then stay there and I'll stay here.

CLEM. You look new.

TONY GOLDILOCKS. I'm in love.

CLEM. You have to try everything once.

TONY GOLDILOCKS. I used to be mad for chaos. There's such a depth of terror. I used to lift its head up by the hair and shake it. You had an un-self-questioning beauty. I wanted to disturb that.

TONY GOLDILOCKS. I followed you when you came here. Found you sleeping in a Soho basement. Chaos all around; screaming prostitutes scaring the morning with their barely covered emotions, mad people with their eyes dangling out, you quietly asleep with a dog like the still centre of the universe. And something happened, I was rearranged in a different order. I'm an idiot now. I'm going to die a wine salesman. Anything to be near you.

CLEM. You used to find me repulsive. What's changed?

TONY GOLDILOCKS. I have.

MRS GOD. Oh! Do you hear that? She's melted a rock.

TONY GOLDILOCKS. The person I used to be, I can barely remember what he was like.

CLEM. He had a thing about breasts.

TONY GOLDILOCKS. Oh?

CLEM. Yes.

TONY GOLDILOCKS. What kind of a thing?

CLEM. One night he described the breasts of all the women
he'd slept with. How each pair had its own personality. The
posh bony Englishwoman with bosoms as bouncy as teenage
cheerleaders. The ones he lifted to his face like a plate and
licked. The woman with one breast which rose from the
flatness like a small dumpy hill in Suffolk he'd like to lie on
for ever. He talked for an hour.

TONY GOLDILOCKS. I'm struggling to recollect. I'm
struggling not to do the obvious thing and deny it. I wonder
if it was intended as a joke on me as much as anything. My
omnivorous appetite.

CLEM. You described them as we lay in bed together.

TONY GOLDILOCKS. The person I used to be? He didn't
consider anyone. He didn't consider anyone his equal. Breasts
were de-individualised and mine. Can you forgive me?

MRS GOD (*very much for the* BIG GOD). How lovely I would
feel if I melted a rock. I'd forgive almost anything.

TONY GOLDILOCKS. Can you forgive me?

CLEM. No. I can't.

   TONY GOLDILOCKS *exits*.

   BAZ *and* STAN *enter, and* TERESA *follows them on*.

BAZ. I provoke her? It's like trying to negotiate peace with a
complicated fucked-up country that explodes in your face
when you say the word peace.

TERESA. She won't let nothing come between her and
shitness. For the sake of shithood she's willing to throw way
love man peace youngness pleasure all a that, and if it makes
her feel shittier so be it.

STAN. Baz. Can I thank you to please go thank you. I want the story in tomorrow's papers to be the charity event for the limbless, not Natty decks Baz.

BAZ. I walk out those doors it's the end. Is that what you want?

STAN. Yes.

> NATTY *enters dressed like a star. She has a heart-shaped diamond clutch which is reminiscent of* MRS GOD's *shitbag.*

NATTY. What d'you think?

> *She displays the dress.*

Does my ego look too big in this? I don't want to amp it up too far, you get me, wanna look like I'm comfortable in my own skin. It's a charity dinner for the limbless. The charity phoned and asked Stan did I want to cancel in the circumstances, because of Mum and that. I was like Stan, who's gonna stand up for the limbless if I don't?

TERESA. The thing is, Natty, iss lovely being charitable but iss not you is it.

NATTY. Who is it then?

TERESA. It's not though is it.

NATTY. Yes it is, Teresa.

TERESA. It's what celebrities do; they get a charity to celebrate their celebrityhood.

NATTY. I know what it's like to be limbless, Teresa. I lost my limbs.

TERESA. I am staring at you in disbelief.

NATTY. It's horrible, I tell ya. It's a horrible thing; I cannot talk without my hands. I couldn't say nothing. Someone should study me, I should donate my brain to Oxford University.

TERESA. Why, they tryna build an idiot?

STAN. We're gonna be well late, Natty. I think we should go babes.

NATTY. We're going, babes.

TERESA. Was the limbless your idea or did Stan suggest it?

NATTY. Stan suggested it. We was talkin bout her mum one
night and she was saying how her mum was limbless and,
tell em what you said, Stan. Made me proper cry.

STAN. I said you wouldn't know I had a mum looking at the
photos I got. It's like she died when I was four or something;
after that all the photos are of me. Thousands of me.

NATTY. See the tabloids won't run a story except they got a
pic. And a charity that can't get pics in the papers cos they
ain't saving kiddies or dogs or pink things, is gonna die of
starvation and fucking ignorance. Thass where I come in. I
got more self-loathing than the limbless people but I'm the
kind a ugly the cameras love.

TERESA. It's a sad reflection on society though innit, the way
you've projectile-vomited to the top.

NATTY. You're quiet, Baz. You got anything to say before you
like bawl out.

BAZ. Not in front of other people.

    Pain yeah?

NATTY. Yes. Pain.

BAZ. Pain is the foundation on which we built this relationship.
Wrong. Pain is the concrete with which we poured the
foundations.

NATTY. Pain yes pain what about pain?

BAZ. Nothing yeah? Nothing.

NATTY. That all you got to say, fucking nothing? That's tragic
that is. I mean we have the privilege to speak the language of
William so-called Shakespeare innit; the least you can do is
aspire to that privilege by saying something English that
we'll remember, you tit. Just quote some Shakespeare if you
can't make nothing up original.

BAZ. Yeah? Like what?

NATTY. Like fucking, food glorious food, hot sausage and mustard. Or that other one. Never in the whole upsetness of human history have so many been twatted by so few.

BAZ. Why I hesitate to discuss violence.

NATTY. Fucking discuss it, man, fucking discuss away to fuck.

BAZ. Hesitate to discuss violence. What concertinas my balls. The paps out there. You inflating like an airbag in a car crash. Before I even. Think of the size of a mind. Sex and violence in a too-small space. Like a mind. Or a bedroom.

NATTY. He's forgotten how we started. First two weeks the sex was raw. He ragsed me. Didn't ya? He done it like he was fresh out of jail and rough as dogs so when he hurt me first time I thought he done it by accident. He clocked I liked it and after that he took it further and further. It was him that switched me on. I didn't know the switch was there even. I would lay on the bed nothing but skin, like a tent on a black dreary moor in Scotland (not that I ever been to Scotland) tent on a black moor that is tied out stiff and quiverin, and arches its back when the wind claws it with its nails. Then lets the rain belt it till iss drenched.

He switched me on.

BAZ. It was too much.

NATTY. It was supposed to be too much.

BAZ. Lately it's got too much too much.

NATTY. How can there be too much too much.

BAZ. It was too real.

This flicks a switch in NATTY *and from this moment she is going to be violent. There is no need for any escalation or change of pace. In fact, in order to get close to* BAZ, *she needs to approach him in a way that doesn't make him back away.*

NATTY. Too real yeah, he says it was too real, I want to be real.

BAZ. It's a thin line between loving someone violently and attacking them.

NATTY. Thin line is it.

BAZ. Thin line yeah.

NATTY. You want to see the thin line? I'll show you the thin –

She kicks BAZ *in the balls.*

– line.

He bends double. He's at her mercy. She has all the time in the world. He's bent over and she holds him by a handful of his hair.

When we done sex I was beside myself in ex– (*Knees him in the face.*) stasies, I was beyond the farthest – (*Knees him.*) place, I was gone to the – (*Knees him.*) mountain top. I was gone.

When BAZ *breaks free of her, his face is streaming blood and* NATTY *stands there with a certain amount of the preening that goes along with victory, the almost-smile.*

TERESA. You're mental you are.

NATTY. Yes I am mental.

BAZ. You're fucked up.

NATTY (*to* BAZ). I am fucked up! Can you fucking handle it?

STAN. That's tomorrow's front page, his face looking like that.

TERESA. That's tomorrow's front page, his face.

NATTY. Tell security to open the gates. Open the fucking gates!

BAZ. how bleeding do I actually am

STAN. can we please find the meantime

NATTY. let them see the raw bleeding me

BAZ. can your ego for one minute think

NATTY. think you think i can have a shit-ectomy. how do i fix this

She means her head.

when I only got this

She indicates her head.

to fix it with

BAZ. you want to drop the bomb

NATTY. drop the fucking bomb

BAZ. this will be a

NATTY. tomic fucking bomb

BAZ. atomic fucking bomb of publicity. blow everything off the front pages and blind *us*. next day yeah, everything fine, children shops traffic. you and me cut from each other like sight from the eyes

The gates open. BAZ exits. A million flashbulbs go off, photographing that bleeding face.

TERESA exits into the house. NATTY passes STAN on the way inside.

NATTY. He was asking for it, Stan.

STAN. I know, babes.

NATTY and STAN exit.

Once she's alone, CLEM goes to the pool of blood where the violence happened.

MRS GOD. she likes the blood.

THE BIG GOD. she likes the blank the blanking, the violence

MRS GOD. does she want to be him, or her. she wants to be all mixed up in it

CLEM exits.

THE BIG GOD. she's double lost. it's like she's on a trip inside a trip.

Music

End of first half.

ACT TWO

Scene One

The funeral of NATTY *and* TERESA*'s mum. A coffin processing through the street and into the church.*

As they walk up the aisle of the church with the coffin they begin to sing: 'I Am So Shit'. NATTY *sings in the first person; the others sing in the third person.*

NATTY.

> I am so shit
> I am so shit
> I'm shit, baby
> I am so shit
> I am so shit
> I'm shit, baby

OTHERS.

> She's so shit
> She's so shit
> She's so shit, baby
> She's so shit
> She' s so shit
> She's so shit, baby

NATTY.

> Please please
> Love me ugly
> Please please
> Love me ugly
> Please

OTHERS.

> Please please
> Love her ugly
> Please please

> Love her ugly
> Please

NATTY.

> Take me back you bastard
> So what if I'm shit?
> I need you so much, I'm
> The one that you hit;
> Oh take me take me back in your arms
> I'm desperate

OTHERS.

> Take her back you bastard
> So what if she's shit?
> She needs you so much, she's
> The one that you hit
> Oh take her take her back in your arms
> She's desperate

NATTY.

> I fill my self with loathing
> I eat till I ache;
> I gorge on the pain
> Get sick like on cake;
> Oh eat me baby keep me awake
> I taste so nice

OTHERS.

> She fills herself with loathing
> She eats till she aches
> She gorges on pain
> Gets sick like on cake;
> Oh eat her baby keep her awake
> She tastes so nice

NATTY.

> Please please
> Love me ugly
> Please please
> Love me ugly
> Please

OTHERS.
>Please please
>Love her ugly
>Please please
>Fucking love her
>Please

Poppies begin to fall.

Scene Two

NATTY, TERESA *and* STAN *enter as though from a church immediately after a funeral mass, full of tears and bravery. Snappers lie in wait for them.*

NATTY. I didn't think I'd cry as much as this.

STAN. It's your mum's funeral, babes.

NATTY. I thought I'd be stronger. Did you cry, Stan?

STAN. I did cry, babes.

TERESA. I cried from start to finish. The priest and the little altar boys all dressed up.

STAN. I cried when all the poppies came down.

NATTY. When the poppy petals floated down on everyone from the ceiling? That was my idea, Stan. She died in battle.

STAN. What job did she do?

NATTY. She was a hospital cleaner. The poppies were a symbol of that. She done one of them jobs you get no respect for when you're alive.

TERESA. She died every day of her life. It was my idea to play that Clash song. 'Career Opportunities'. I wanted that.

BAZ *and* CLEM *enter.*

STAN. Look who's here.

TERESA. Was he in the church? He's a hypocrite coming here after spreading his slapped-up face all over the papers. He made you look like a proper gypsy.

CLEM (*to* BAZ). She asked to see you but she probably has to pretend different. D'you mind talking to her in public?

BAZ. No man, it'll be more private in public. In the bedroom she acts like she has to project herself or the public won't know what she's feeling.

CLEM *goes up to* NATTY.

CLEM. Natty. He just wants to offer his condolences he says.

NATTY. If he wants to offer his condolences.

NATTY *and* BAZ *move away from the others to have a private conversation where nobody can hear them, except for the entire audience. Should feel like the audience are in on a very private moment.*

Summing terrible has happened yeah and nobody else I can trust. Most people only tell you what you wanna hear else they get fired.

Thing is yeah. Do people look down on me? I mean the press and the public and that, do they all look down on me?

BAZ. Who told you that?

TERESA. The car's waiting for us, Natty.

BAZ. Did Teresa tell you that?

Yes, she did.

NATTY. I need to know, Baz. Do people think I'm shit? You can tell me the truth. I know I ain't got no talent. I never said I had talent. I thought that's why they liked me because none of them's got talent either so they can identify with me. I thought I was a model to people of what you can achieve when you ain't got nothing except your positivity.

Turns out they think I'm a cartoon. I don't want them taking pictures of me no more. It's like asking me to take off my clothes then having a laugh. What's wrong with them? Why do they wanna put shit on a pedestal for?

BAZ. They loathe themselves.

NATTY. They what themselves? *Loathe* themselves.

BAZ. And the best thing in the world if you don't wanna change is looking down on someone else. They find someone they think they can look down on they heave a sigh of relief and let their bellies flop out. Nothing they like better than a good crisis. That's a big fat takeaway that is. We put it all out there man. We wade the shit marshes. We go on voyages to like *shit knows*. The seas swallow us up and spew us up on a desert African shore where some lion licks us into life. They drive the kids to ballet classes. They gotta take it out on someone.

This is why NATTY *loves the guy. He's a genius.*

NATTY. Will you come in the car to the cemetery?

BAZ. Yeah.

TERESA. It's just that I feel bad keeping everyone waiting, Natty.

NATTY (*to* BAZ). You ready for this?

They exit. The snappers go mental and follow after them.

STAN *and* TERESA *are suddenly left behind.*

STAN. Look at the paps.

TERESA. It's like there was a landslide. The world suddenly moved twenty yards along the road.

STAN. They are loving this.

TERESA. One minute I was here, the next nothing was here.

STAN. If I was your publicist, I couldn't get you arrested right now. D'you know anyone who can give us a lift?

TERESA. We better ask Uncle Mike and Auntie Carol.

They exit.

Scene Three

TONY GOLDILOCKS *enters and talks to the audience.*

TONY GOLDILOCKS. I've been thinking about when you hurt someone badly like I've done...

...and what it means to hurt someone...

...and the fact we do hurt...

...and...

...I mean when was the last time you forgave someone who hurt you badly. Your father daughter mother husband ex. You don't do you. You want to punish them for what they did and if you forgave them it would be like letting the bastards off. Sometimes you *say* you've forgiven them – after about a decade – because if you go on about it for two decades people might mistake you for the unforgiving type. So you say you've forgiven them or you say you don't give a fuck about them; by which you mean you nurse a resentment at a sub-murderous level where it won't be too visible to anyone, primarily yourself.

The funeral reception. There is light, well-dressed security at the door. TONY GOLDILOCKS *is on this side of the security barrier, shut out. He tries to attract someone's attention.*

SECURITY WOMAN. Can I help you, sir? This is a private function...

TONY GOLDILOCKS. I'm looking for someone.

SECURITY WOMAN. We're not usually allowed to say piss off but I'm leaving tomorrow.

TONY GOLDILOCKS. Look, there, she's coming.

CLEM *comes out to see him.*

CLEM. What are you doing here?

TONY GOLDILOCKS. I was in the hotel on business.

CLEM. You followed me to a funeral?

TONY GOLDILOCKS. I'm desperate!

I know you can't forgive me but I want you to know I'm ashamed of how arrogant I was. I thought I knew it all. I thought I was right about everything. I thought I rode the edge of time. And what I've learned is that some things are sacred. You, for instance. Yes, all this moment of illumination has done is light up the moving carpet of cockroaches that was my conscience and my soul... but I'm still sort of glad to know what I'm made of.

CLEM. When you say some things are sacred, does that mean some things are sacred and some are not?

TONY GOLDILOCKS. I suppose so, yes.

CLEM. And do you decide which is which? Gardens but not slugs; the universe but not Essex; black people but not nail salons?

TONY GOLDILOCKS. I don't think I don't intend any arrogance. It's an individual thing. We each of us have to decide what's sacred.

CLEM. Whether I'm sacred or not is not your decision, is it? I'm pleased you're rethinking things but the fact that mentally you've moved me from one category to another reminds me that you like to order the world and the things in it, and I don't like to be in any category of your mind.

BAZ *enters.*

BAZ. Clem, can I have a word with you?

CLEM (*going to* BAZ). So, what were you and Natty up to in the ladies'? You were ages in there.

BAZ. We had an insanely serious talk and we've decided to give it another go.

CLEM. Awww. She's so lucky. I'm so glad. She's so so lucky. I'm so so glad.

BAZ. Yeah fly out to Berlin a couple couple of days. Berlin's nuts and sort of cool and a bit avant-gardish, we thought we'd get an hotel and experiment with like sex stripped right back to its bare essentials. Two people fucking.

CLEM. None of the paraphernalia.

BAZ. No items.

CLEM. Naked sex? Wow. I'd love that. That would be so interesting.

TONY GOLDILOCKS *exits*.

BAZ. The thing is, the reason I'm telling you, she wants her bag back with the fetish stuff. She doesn't want the stuff. She just wants it *back*.

CLEM. You don't think she might have a double motive?

BAZ. You think she might have a double motive?

CLEM. She might not even know it. She might be thinking in all innocence she means what she says.

BAZ. Yeah.

CLEM. Do you think you've got a double motive?

BAZ. While we're away in Berlin, can you get the bag back? I'm asking you to do this for *me,* man. And then like mind your own business. Can you do that?

CLEM. Yes. Course I can.

BAZ. Cheers, man.

He goes. There has been a certain speed and brutality about the way he's got what he wanted and that leaves her a bit crushed.

Scene Four

The BIG GOD *and* MRS GOD *enter.*

THE BIG GOD. Where's she gone? Where is the mad cow?

MRS GOD. I'm here.

THE BIG GOD. I can't see you if you stand on that side of me,
I told you that.

MRS GOD. You told me no such thing.

THE BIG GOD. I said I'm a cliff on that side.

MRS GOD. Don't remember you saying you were a cliff.

THE BIG GOD. I told you this is my dangerous cliff side.
Large pieces of my mind suddenly collapse into the sea.

MRS GOD. Are there things you would like to say to people
before you forget who they are?

THE BIG GOD. There's a giant rubbling around the ruins of

fucking despair

And I tell you another thing. He's a thief. That's the
interesting. He's broken the jewels out of all the necklaces
and scattered them around the

yes, and if I found some I could put them on a sequence of
events and take her home.

EDWARDO *enters and finds the Hermès Kelly bag where he
buried it, somewhere on or under the stage; he buried it
wrapped in the final edition of the* News of the World.

EDWARDO. I tell you what I have in common with celebrities
and stars and that, a lack of privacy. This – (*The space in his
head.*) is the most densely populated square foot in London.
The voices yeah? Don't matter where I am or what I'm doing.
Yesterday this utter random crept into my head and said:

(*Exceedingly depressed and dreary Scottish voice, like a rainy Sabbath day on the Isle of Lewis.*) Can I interest you in the purchase of some Scottish wine? This is an effervescent sparkling wine made from a grape which is grown on south-west facing slopes outside Cowdenbeath, in the traditional Scottish rain. Scottish wine is passionate yet intriguing and highly sought after for its unusual flavour; furthermore, each bottle comes with a unique guarantee that nobody has urinated in the contents. I said I don't know why you're talking to me, yeah, I'm allergic to wine. Do your fucking research.

I'm overrun with voices. I have to stay awake when I'm sleeping to keep guard else more of them will move in.

THE BIG GOD. Sleep? I never sleep. If I came across Sleep I would fuck her and sleep for a thousand years.

EDWARDO. I dream about sleep.

THE BIG GOD. If I was in the world I could sleep over there curled up on a piece of pavement. Here I'm boundless, infinite, unending, I go on and on.

EDWARDO. Yes, you fucking do, mate. Will you please eff off and leave me alone?

THE BIG GOD. Have you got any idea who I am? I'm God. I'm the God of this universe.

EDWARDO (*he only hears the* BIG GOD, *he never sees him*). Oh man. The God delusion. Edwardo, you are letting yourself down, mate. How low have I sunk?

THE BIG GOD. How low have *you* sunk?

EDWARDO. I tell the psychiatrists I'm a God-hearer they will condone me to being a joke for three months and beat in my brains with big thick drugs. Leave me alone, man, I am not going back to mental hospital until winter.

THE BIG GOD. Is this what I've come to. I'm a voice in a mental person's head.

MRS GOD. Don't look down on him, he's a toe-hold on reality.

THE BIG GOD. Fucking frostbitten toe-hold.

MRS GOD. Talk to him.

THE BIG GOD. Edwardo, I'm a big *knob*...

MRS GOD. You mean, you're a *big* knob...

THE BIG GOD. I don't talk to every Tom Dick or Harry.

EDWARDO. Oh, man. He's come to tell me I'm special. Got any instructions commandments, people you want me to kill?

THE BIG GOD. Don't tempt me.

CLEM *and* TERESA *enter.*

CLEM. Edwardo? Did you find the bag?

TERESA. You ain't nothing without that bag, Edwardo. Give it back and you are sleeping on pavements again.

CLEM. It's not ours though is it.

TERESA. I'm not bothered about me. I'm thinking about him. Must be hard living on the streets, people laughing at ya. You must feel well shit about yourself.

EDWARDO *hands the bag to* CLEM.

EDWARDO. It's just sex things. It's just sex at the end of the day. There's things locked up in the cells of the body and when you have sex all those things are let out of jail.

CLEM *and* TERESA *exit.*

THE BIG GOD. Edwardo, I have a daughter. Can you pass on a message from God?

EDWARDO. Are you insane? *People take me seriously.*

You need help.

EDWARDO *exits.*

THE BIG GOD. The cliff has just collapsed.

The BIG GOD *exits after* EDWARDO. MRS GOD *follows.*

Scene Five

A hotel bedroom in Berlin. A bed pushed onto the stage.

BAZ *and* NATTY *have tried twice already to have straight non-fetishistic sex. It has not gone well. They are on a break. BAZ is reading a book. NATTY has a remote control in her hand and is channel-hopping with half an eye on (we imagine) a plasma screen. She is wearing a nightdress; he is in trousers and bare chest.*

NATTY. I am not happy, Baz. The only part about loathing myself I use to like was the sex we use to have and now for some reason we got to give that up.

BAZ. You're having a baby.

NATTY. Does that have to ruin the shit out of everything else *as well*. I don't know why you brought me here, Baz. It's hideous. Can we go home? Baz, can we go home? Baz, can we go home?

BAZ. touch each other, Natty. touch each other. how to touch each other. you take some day-long flight yeah your skin feels like the inside of a hoover bag, you don't want anyone near you. that's all. we're between two places. we use to touch each other one way, we got to try and find a new (   ) a new (fucking) modality

NATTY. We've been doing it for two hours. I'm sore trying.

BAZ. We are not leaving this room till we can do normal sex and enjoy it.

NATTY. Please, Baz. Love me ugly. Please.

BAZ. What's that noise?

NATTY. That noise? That's the carnival.

The carnival enters with music and goes right through their bedroom, carnivalising it. The carnival is a chance to unify some images from earlier – angels and demons, a dead doctor rising out of a coffin and offering poisonous-looking medicine, transvestites and sexiness. The carnival exits.

I tell you what I like about England. The telly. Are we gonna have sex or not?

BAZ *puts his book down.*

BAZ. Yes we are going to have sex. Get on the bed.

NATTY (*assuming the doggy position on the bed*). I'm in such a bad mood, Baz. I'm in a militant cow of a mood.

BAZ. Do you want a punch on the lips?

NATTY. Do you want a punch on the lips? I'm in tears and we haven't even started.

She's not in tears.

BAZ. You are not in tears.

NATTY. Yes I am in tears, Baz, believe me. Keep your trousers on. I like the roughness of the zip and the stud.

He goes inside her from behind without any niceties or preamble. It's sore. It hurts and they both like that. But then it settles down to in out in out in out in out. This goes on a long time.

Do you think I should have my arse done?

BAZ. No.

NATTY. Is it too square?

BAZ. No.

NATTY. What's wrong with it then?

BAZ. Nothing wrong with it.

NATTY. It's not doing nothing for you. It's a flippin insult how long you're taking.

BAZ. Look, I'm not enjoying this either yeah. That's nature; you don't see dogs doing it with a smile on their face.

Sex continues.

Hard to get beneath the surface.

NATTY. That cistern keeps hissing.

I tell you what this is like. This is like the war. They use to eat things like powdered eggs. And cakes that had no butter in them. Everything was pretend. A cake was just enough like a cake to be annoyin. That's what this is like.

BAZ. Did you ask Stan to get me an egg-mayonnaise sandwich?

NATTY. Yes.

What's your book about?

BAZ (*punctuated with rhythmic thrusting and smacking noises and his difficult breathing*). The philosophy of the mind and artificial intelligence. Whether a computer will ever be able to think or have a mind like a human. A mathematician called Alan Turing devised a test for computers called The Imitation Game.

NATTY. I heard a that.

BAZ. The idea is yeah if a computer can pass itself off as a human then it's got a mind like a human. And the test is, can it hold an intelligent conversation for five minutes?

NATTY. Why make things harder for computers. Thass discrimination that is. How many people can hold an intelligent conversation for five minutes? I tell you a better test. Can it have like a totally stupid conversation?

Sex continues.

BAZ. I'm not going to come. Are you?

NATTY. No.

BAZ. Will we stop?

NATTY. Yeah.

He goes on fucking her, sad.

BAZ. I love you, I love you, I love you, I love you, I love you, I love you, I love you, I love you...

He keeps saying this over and over. Eventually he is saying it and fucking her kind of hard – hard and angry and almost crying with frustration. He stops, zips up.

Post-sex BAZ and NATTY don't say anything for a while. They consider their situation.

These days when I'm smoking weed it's like I'm in a wood, yeah. It's raining and I'm as sad as a dead log. I know nothing's going to change until the log rots.

NATTY. I want to *change,* Baz. I just don't want to be *different* to the way we are.

STAN *enters. She's been out there in the carnival, so there should be some visual trace of that.*

STAN. Knock knock.

NATTY. Look who it is.

STAN. It's bonkers out there.

BAZ. Did you get my egg-mayonnaise sandwich.

STAN. Oh I forgot.

BAZ (*somewhere darker than despair*). You forgot my egg-mayonnaise sandwich?

NATTY. We could get a proper egg-mayonnaise sandwich in England. Let's leave tomorrow morning, Baz.

STAN. Oh. Can I come?

NATTY. Stan, can you stop being a facade? Look at ya. You got the timeless chic wool suit, the Loriblu ankle boots, the maroon tights; what is up with you? You cannot keep a man for two secs. You go on holiday with your clients. You're like an imitation. You got to change, girl. We all have. We can't make an exception for *you* just cos you're an idiot.

STAN. The last boyfriend, his mother died. I didn't know what to do to help him. I said, tell me what to do! He didn't know either. He couldn't tell me.

Can I come to bed with you tonight?

NATTY. Can Stan come to bed with us tonight? Course you can, babes.

They all end up on the bed, the total opposite in every way of a sexual threesome. BAZ hands round a spliff.

The bed is pushed off the stage.

Scene Six

Essex house. Swimming pool. Decked out like for a pool party. EDWARDO enters. He opens a bottle of wine and pours it into the swimming pool.

TERESA enters. She is already soaked and she has a bottle of white spirits in her hand. Her mood is weirdly up.

EDWARDO. I got three hundred and nineteen illnesses, which is interesting yeah because three hundred and nineteen is a very unbalanced number.

TERESA. Since she come back from Berlin she cannot stop sacking people. Her eyes keep spinning like a fruit machine and they keep like missing the jackpot.

She's even sacked Stan. She's even sacked her publicist.

Yeah. My life and hers. Thing is. I done a lot of different things in my time. Did I tell you I used to be a lap dancer. I smashed it as a dancer, you're lovely when you're young innit. When I got on a bit I got breast enlargements, to keep up with the younger girls? I had three of them before I stopped.

Look. Found some white spirits in that shed.

She pours a bottle of white spirits over herself. The feeling behind this is at least in part one of superbness, like having a secret power or protection.

Tingles nips, not so bad as I thought it would, like when you get stung by nettles and you go numb.

She sings, like she's having a shower.

> Take a bath in me, baby
> Sink down into me, baby
> Have a large drink, maybe
> Take a deep breath and
> Go right under;
> Go right under go right under
> Go right under.

EDWARDO. That was interesting. Yes. You are *Jesus* mental. I'm keeping my eyes on you.

TERESA. I'm looking forward to Natty's face when I set myself alight. She'll be sort of extinguished.

She has a sudden panic.

I hope I ain't soaked my fags. (S*he gets them out, sees they are fine.*) Thank goodness for that.

She lights a fag and smokes with a certain amount of care, seeing as she's flammable.

She's gonna tell us to leave today, I can feel it. She's gonna make us homeless. I ain't trying to make a point or nothing. So long as she's happy, know what I mean? So long as she's contented. I'm doing this as a spiritual thing. It's like who are we anyway? We come from oblivion and to oblivion we shall return, and with what measure we conduct ourselves is how we shall be measured.

TERRY CASH *enters with crate of beers and* TONY GOLDILOCKS *with wine.*

TERRY CASH. You picked a perfect day to turn up. It's mad here. How much for the wine?

TONY GOLDILOCKS. Fifty quid a bottle.

TERRY CASH. I'll take six.

He flashes the cash.

I've been sacked. Binned. She flew home from Berlin no sleep started axing people left right and centre. Blood everywhere. So we're having a party to celebrate. What's the wine?

TONY GOLDILOCKS. It's a Condrieu, 2007, Yves Cuilleron vineyard, nose a bit like toasted something, tastes of dry fruit with a hint of flowers.

TERRY CASH. You say that like you've never tasted it, open your mouth roll it over your tongue. I am going to cook you the best steak you ever had, sesame oil rice wine pear marinade, will be dribbling down your jaw – all you have to do is enjoy it. Look at your garms, you're too smooth – you've got the soul of a cocktail pianist. You've got the personality of a square plate. You're as tight as a slightly runny arse. I'll lend you some swimming shorts and a T-shirt.

TONY GOLDILOCKS. That's very generous of you but I don't swim can't swim.

TERRY CASH. You surprise me.

TONY GOLDILOCKS. I don't like being out of my depth.

TERRY CASH. I'm sorry, mate, you're going in.

He picks TONY *up and threatens to drop him in the pool.* TONY *screeches.*

TONY GOLDILOCKS. No, I can't swim I can't swim I can't swim I can't swim.

TERRY CASH *puts him down.*

TERRY CASH. Jesus shit. Open the wine, I'll get an ice bucket.

TERRY CASH *and* TONY GOLDILOCKS *exit.*

By this time TERESA *is sitting in the sun.* EDWARDO *is keeping her in view, maybe from behind a pillar. He has a chopping knife he's taken from barbecue cutlery.*

NATTY *enters*.

The idea behind the following dialogue is that it arises out of a dizzily hot day. While taking in the world from behind sunglasses, NATTY *and* TERESA *let their words drift up and off like balloons…*

TERESA.…we ain't got your bag if thass what you think…

NATTY.…change…

TERESA.…sunbathing, where do you go? lost continent. somewhere under…

…am i sizzling? can you hear me sizzle over there?…

NATTY.…Mum used to say, I just wish Teresa could be happy.

TERESA.…here in millionaire Essex. all the nouveaux *cunts*. i wish you all the love in the world, babes…

NATTY.…so long as you got your family innit…

TERESA.…the thing about spirituality people forget, people forget it's just another word for breathing…

NATTY.…Mum used to say, she could start a row in an empty house that Teresa.…

TERESA.… know what you're *really* like…

NATTY.…come back any time…

TERESA *gets half up*.

TERESA.…you throwing me out are ya?

NATTY.…no hurry, sweets… any time today is fine…

TERESA *stands*.

TERESA.…if you could see my hidden thoughts…

EDWARDO.…she unveiled herself to me…

NATTY.…she's a mystery to me, i'm glad to say. i hope she stays that way…

TERESA....it's either you or me, Natty. there can only be one
of us.

You remember them words, girl...

EDWARDO....they'll be famous them words...

TERESA....i'm gonna cool off a bit. i been pouring

TERESA *mimes 'pouring white spirits over her head'*.

over my head. it's like when Mum remember used to put a
damp cloth on your forehead when you was sick. it cools my
soul.

TERESA *exits,* NATTY *exits*.

EDWARDO *exits with the knife he has picked up*.

TONY GOLDILOCKS *enters separately – with something
for the poolside party*.

CLEM *enters, preoccupied with the Hermès Kelly bag she's
holding and its contents*.

CLEM. There's a figure of speech where you take the part for the
whole so like, famous one, friends, romans, countrymen, lend
me your ears, when he doesn't want their ears he wants their
attention or when you say about someone, he's very fond of
the bottle, and you mean he likes the contents of the bottle.
Well, seems all sorts of people fall in love with the bottle.

TONY GOLDILOCKS. Still angry with me.

CLEM. I'm not angry.

TONY GOLDILOCKS. You are angry.

CLEM. I don't care enough to be angry.

TONY GOLDILOCKS. I hear myself talk about some wine, the
maker, the nose. It's like I'm ghosting someone. I'm
ghosting around. You know when you pass a swimming pool
on a miserable wet day. It's all like that.

CLEM. Without love where's the tension? There's no suspense.
Everything sags. I'm surprised people can bear being human.

TONY GOLDILOCKS. If you could admit you're furious with me you might be a lot happier.

TERRY CASH *has entered in the background and lifts* TONY GOLDILOCKS *up as though to dump him in the pool, and* TONY GOLDILOCKS *screams*.

Stop, it's not funny, stop, it's not funny.

TERRY *puts him down*.

Nothing amusing about it, I can't swim.

TERRY CASH. I never said it were funny. Help me with the salads.

TERRY CASH *and* TONY GOLDILOCKS *exit*.

TERESA *enters, even more soaked in white spirits*. EDWARDO *is behind her*.

TERESA. Natty's coming to get her bag.

EDWARDO. Natty's coming to get her bits and pieces.

NATTY *and* BAZ *enter*.

BAZ. the bag. what can I say? this is what it's all about.

NATTY. ss not about a bag, Baz.

BAZ. about the contents of the bag.

NATTY. not about the contents neither.

BAZ. the bag has mixed us all up. anguish pain love loathing sex sisters dogs. we got to tease out who's who and who's not. and separate or try to work out what needs to be separated if it comes to it.

CLEM. Natty. this for me has been a journey. long long road to. take my leave. find, i have found the, definitely, found the, that i came for.

She holds out the bag.

to wear a whipped back and to bring someone a whip

hoping

that

i hope the two of you are very happy together

BAZ. let's bury the bag in the centre of the earth where it belongs

NATTY. we can't bury the bag, Baz

BAZ. go and get a spade

CLEM *exits*.

NATTY. she's only gone to get a spade

BAZ. we can bury the contents. ss just the remains

NATTY. what d'you mean iss just the remains. ss the remains, Baz

BAZ. i'm agreeing with you. remains

NATTY. remains, Baz

BAZ. i know. i know.

NATTY. the remains is all we've got, Baz

CLEM *enters*

CLEM. i got a spade

NATTY. sweet Mary Jesus. it's not a pet hamster. i ain't seven. i don't believe in hamster heaven. Baz, you fucking, we are going to look like a proper pair of tom-toms burying summing in the garden. is she going to stand there holding that spade?

BAZ. it's like why not do it as a sort of ritual ritualistic thing yeah?

NATTY. because it's pretend thass why. it's pretend play-acting, it's stupid

BAZ. if you can't even bury the shit when it's pretending

NATTY. i ain't gonna do stupid pretending in front of everyone watching

BAZ. just act it. just act burying the shit. and see if you can do it.

TERESA. he's making you small, Natty. i keep telling ya, do not try and be someone else. what the public love about you is your authenticness. you got this ever-blazin anger – ain't since you become a celebrity – even when you was a girl – on the street n that – you was always losing your temper. that was your swagger. and when you explode you expand like the universe done and that is the reason i am like a nothing and you are a personality. your anger is your tiara girl. you become like a nice girl we won't know who she is. be yourself, Natty. blaze. blow these cunts off the face of the earth

NATTY *picks up the bag. She looks inside it.*

is everythin there aright?

NATTY *throws the bag to* TERESA.

NATTY. you keep it. nothing to me. change it for money.

TERRY CASH *and other* PARTY PEOPLE *come out to spectate.*

TERESA. I ain't important, I know that much. Ain't got nothing cept my dignity and thass hard sometimes to keep that. Do I look cool? I look cool innit.

She lights a fag.

I found bottles of white spirit in a shed today and soaked myself didn't I.

EDWARDO. She poured them over her head and sang.

TERESA. It's sad, Natty, you thinking what I want is money. Ain't the material things in life, it's the respect.

NATTY. I know what you want, Teresa, you want to be me. You doing this for publicity? You want some publicity? You jealous of the publicity I get?

BAZ. Natty.

NATTY. She don't frighten me. I don't believe her anyway. She's gobby but she won't do nothing.

TERESA *walks towards them smoking and with a lighter in hand, like she will set alight to herself and take one of them with her. Again there is an element of superbness about this – like she's enjoying the power of it. They all move away from her, not taking any chances; except for* EDWARDO *who follows right behind her.*

TERESA. Do *you* believe me? Do *you* believe me? Do *you* believe me?

They evidently do.

I tell you why I'm so believable. I do not have the money for the bus home and a person that don't have the money for their bus home and don't have a home in the first place don't think like anyone else. You think you know what I'm going to do you're wrong cos I don't know what I'm going to do. I never knew I was this fucking nuts. I'm free, Natty. Thass the difference between me and you. I ain't trapped in the illusion of reality like you are.

BAZ. Teresa, I'm reaching out to you, man. Help me. Give me something. I just want everyone to come to the party know what I'm saying. It's like a bad-made spliff. If it only burns up one side nobody enjoys it. So what I would ask you to do, can I ask you to reconfigure your model. You're confusing metaphors. You're not a statement you're a person. You ever see someone burn? They burn as bad as plastic.

NATTY. She don't understand what product she is. She never read the instructions on the box.

TERESA. I ain't doing this for myself, Natty. I'm doing it to show you. This is what you are like.

NATTY. I ain't nothing like you, girl. I ain't nothing like her, am I, Baz?

TERESA. You don't let no one close. They say summing you don't like you go up in flames at them. And yeah you're getting attention you're getting attention you're getting a lot of attention yeah, but you will keep the attention only so long, and only so long *as* know what I mean. They want you to climb out of the wreck get right back into a car and crash it into a fucking tree. Funny thing is, I'm the same now, I'm the same as you. Can't back out now, even suppose I wanted to, have to go through with it now. Got to give the audience what they come for.

EDWARDO. You got to burn the rubbish, Teresa.

TERESA. I ain't someone that chats big and then don't perform. I'm uncompromising, yeah.

NATTY. This is stupid, Teresa.

TERESA. It's not stupid, Natty. I wouldn't call it stupid. Futile, yes. And I can accept the futility but what's annoying the shit out of me, I can see myself performing all these melodramatics and I know none of it's not even original and if you think it is easy to be a cliché truss me it is agony. For me to be a cliché is fucking *unacceptable*. So I apologise for the hideousness of the atrocity and the rubbishness of it, but this is all I've got.

TERESA *is about to set herself alight when* EDWARDO *cuts his wrists and whoops like slashing your wrists is fun. He is spraying the blood around and trying to tell by the reactions of other people whether this is serious or not.*

EDWARDO. brighter than blood, nothing brighter than blood, nothing brighter than blood, nothing brighter than blood, man

The others try and save him and get him off the stage. All exit.

Scene Seven

It's night of the same day. Inside there's a party going on; TERRY CASH*'s party.*

CLEM *enters skulking. Wanting to hide in the garden.*

The BIG GOD *enters, and* MRS GOD.

THE BIG GOD. Yes. Same thing must have occurred to you. How do you act? I'll tell you how you act terror. You keep still. You keep still as a mouse while the eagle drops hoping it won't see you, and when you know it's seen you, you keep even stiller. That's terror.

MRS GOD. All the blood. The pieces. Nothing for us here.

THE BIG GOD. If only a sub-cross section of your brain works can your (word i've just said, i've just said it)

CLEM. brain

THE BIG GOD. brain can your brain survive?

CLEM. No.

THE BIG GOD. I can get on a lot bastarding better without it. It's no use when you're dying is it.

CLEM. Help.

MRS GOD. She can hear us.

CLEM. Look at me skulking. Teresa gone, Edwardo. Me next. They'll find me here sooner or later. I won't be able to face them.

MRS GOD. He's still here. The wine salesman.

CLEM. I *want* to forgive him. But then he starts talking.

MRS GOD. She can't forgive him. Look what I've had to put

up with. You'll know all about it when you've been mis –
(blank) when you've been under when they have malingered
with your feelings

Made unfair

Married you they married you

Again and again!

And the children

Like he didn't care!

Like leftovers.

Right under your nose

All over the rug

The length and breadth of it

The size

Stallion thundering in the fields of joy

The size of the promises, the stubbornness of the stains.

CLEM *is not unsympathetic but this is her mother and it's
her mother naked. She walks away.*

CLEM. You asking me to do what you've done?

MRS GOD (*to the* BIG GOD). On you go. You try. (*To* CLEM.)
He's lost his he's missing some vital piece of information.
Ever seen a goat butting a fence like it would rather beat its
brains out than be a goat – that's your father.

THE BIG GOD. Only way home.

Don't blank yourself out.

Don't prison

Prison bars the mind

Look for the blank, the butter

The butter the butter, don't blank me like I'm blank the
butter!

The smack of the blank

The breath of the

(gone)

The arrangement of the parts

The blank of the brain

The unstoppability of the tears when you fucking yeah?

Don't blank it till it's too late, it'll be too blank by then. The blankness will blanket the blank.

Fucking love love love fuck.

MRS GOD (*to the* BIG GOD). You could always set an example.

(*To* CLEM.) He never even looks at me.

THE BIG GOD. Not since I had that dream. I saw the face of God and it wasn't mine. It was blinding.

CLEM. Whose face did you see?

MRS GOD. Mine?

Yes, he saw hers. He's not going to come right out and say that though.

Turn around and look at me.

He can't do it.

I've been beside you every step of the way.

He still can't do it. He exits.

All the ones she sacked are having a party. They've got a room for coke, a room for weed and a room for sex, nobody's in the room for sex. Tony's trying to have a conversation with a nineteen-year-old girl about laying down some wines.

CLEM *exits inside.* MRS GOD *goes too, choosing her own exit.*

NATTY *enters.*

BAZ *enters the balcony, with his guitar. Neither him nor NATTY are at the party.*

BAZ. What you doing, Natty?

NATTY. I can't sleep.

BAZ. I'm writing a song for you.

Yeah. Writing a song.

Listen to those birds. Four in the morning, manic. Like they've been up all night doing charlie. Me me me me me me me. The presence behind them. The silence.

NATTY. Baz. Am I like Teresa?

BAZ (*seriously.*) Yes you are.

NATTY. I'm serious, Baz. Do I resemble Teresa the smallest little bit?

BAZ. Yes.

NATTY. I mean it, Baz. Tell me the fucking ugly truth! Am I as angry as she is?

BAZ *hits a chord on the guitar. She exits, through the people in the yard. She is hurt by the revelation – needs time to accept she is not who she thought she was.*

CLEM *enters with* TONY GOLDILOCKS.

CLEM. Night.

TONY GOLDILOCKS. Yes.

CLEM. Stars.

TONY GOLDILOCKS. Yes.

She gets naked. I don't mind if her nakedness is done by non-realistic means.

CLEM. I've never had a single romantic feeling in all my life. What do I mean by that? I suppose, when I was goddess of love I was very rich and very practical. Nothing I wanted ever took long. But I've learned a lot. Now I know that love is poor. It sleeps in doorways and pavements. It begs if it has to. Next time you see a beggar? That's your soul when it's desperate. It's not pretty. It's not ugly either. It's practical. It does what it has to do to get what it wants.

She goes down into the pool.

I'm naked as a frog.

TONY GOLDILOCKS. Naked as a cry in the night.

CLEM. Bollock naked.

You coming in?

TONY GOLDILOCKS. That's the deep end.

CLEM. Yes. I want you to jump.

He considers this.

TONY GOLDILOCKS. I've stopped dividing people into sacred and *not* scared.

CLEM. You've stopped dividing people into sacred and not *sacred.*

TONY GOLDILOCKS. Yes. Sacred, and what you said. It's not the night or the stars or the frogs or barbed wire or death that's sacred. It's how I think at moments like this.

He jumps like jumping off a cliff into the darkness.

He can't swim. So he doesn't surface. Neither of them do.

BAZ *comes out with his guitar. He tunes it, picks at it, etc....*

BAZ. Natty. She could have turned you to stone. She screamed at you with a hundred hissing snakes streaming from her hair. You glimpsed the resemblance. You can't look her straight in the face or she will turn you to stone. You have to glimpse her. You gotta glimpse the resemblance. Then you can use it. You're out there in the dark now studying it. And the fact you are studying the resemblance, that's what makes the difference.

Here's the song I wrote for you. You got to imagine the production. Right, here the fuck goes.

He sings his song – 'Tonight My Girlfriend'.

Tonight my girlfriend went and bought
A semi-automatic gun;
When all our battles we have fought
We will shoot the stars for fun

NATTY *appears.*

Tonight the moon is naked white
Tonight my girlfriend has a gun;
Let's go bathe my darling one
In the deep end of the night

Let's go lay down on the grass
In that field beside the sea
Rest your sweet and weary ass
Where there's no you and there's no me;
Yes, all our dreams we will surpass
When we learn to be no
Learn to be no
Learn to be nobody

The melody is continued by a single instrument.

They kiss. The kiss is everything. Sexy scared needy intimate; the beginnings of something.

That's the end of the play.